JEWISH
MIGRATIONS

Jill Rutter

Wayland

Titles in the Migrations series

African Migrations
Chinese Migrations
Indian Migrations
Jewish Migrations

First published in 1994 by Wayland (Publishers) Ltd
61 Western Road, Hove, East Sussex, BN3 1JD, England

© Copyright 1994 Wayland (Publishers) Ltd

Editor: Cath Senker
Picture researcher: Geraldine Nicholls
Series design: Suzie Hooper
Book design: Pardoe Blacker Ltd
Cover design: Simon Borrough
Production controller: Janet Slater

British Library Cataloguing in Publication Data
Rutter, Jill
Jewish Migrations (Migrations series)
I. Title   II. Series
304.80956

ISBN 0-7502-1228-4

Printed and bound in Italy by G. Canale & C.S.P.A., Turin

Links with the National Curriculum

HISTORY

KS 2 Core Unit 4: Britain since 1930
KS 3 Core Unit 4: The Twentieth-Century World –
The Second World War, including the Holocaust.
Also the rise of National Socialism in Germany; Hitler.

GEOGRAPHY

KS 2 Communications: Journeys
KS 3 Population: Migration

The cross-curricular theme of Citizenship, particularly
component 2: A Pluralist Society, and also component 3:
Being a Citizen.

Teachers may also wish to use this book in religious
education and social studies. It can be used as a
background reader to set books such as *The Diary of
Anne Frank*.

While every effort has been made to secure permission, in some
cases it has proved impossible to trace copyright holders. The
publishers apologise for this apparent negligence.

CONTENTS

Note on dates

The modern Christian calendar has been used in this book. This calendar is now used in everyday life in Israel.

BC (Latin for Before Christ) is not used in this book. Instead BCE (Before Common Era) is used for BC. CE (Christian Era) is used in chapter 3 instead of AD (Anno Domini, or After Christ).

The Jewish Population today

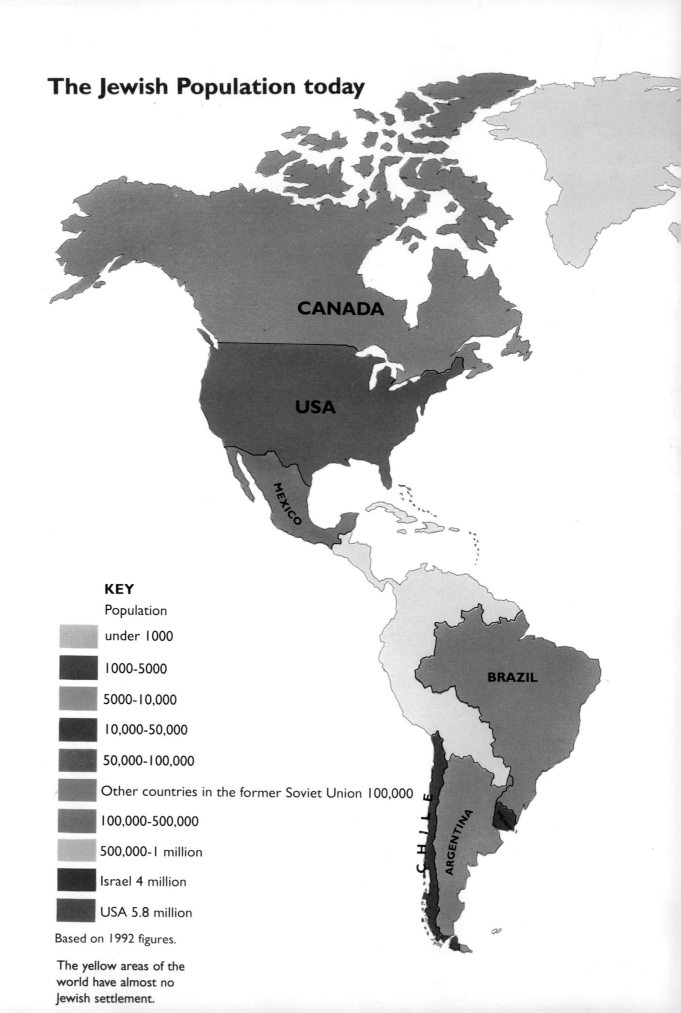

CANADA

USA

MEXICO

BRAZIL

CHILE

ARGENTINA

KEY

Population

under 1000

1000-5000

5000-10,000

10,000-50,000

50,000-100,000

Other countries in the former Soviet Union 100,000

100,000-500,000

500,000-1 million

Israel 4 million

USA 5.8 million

Based on 1992 figures.

The yellow areas of the world have almost no Jewish settlement.

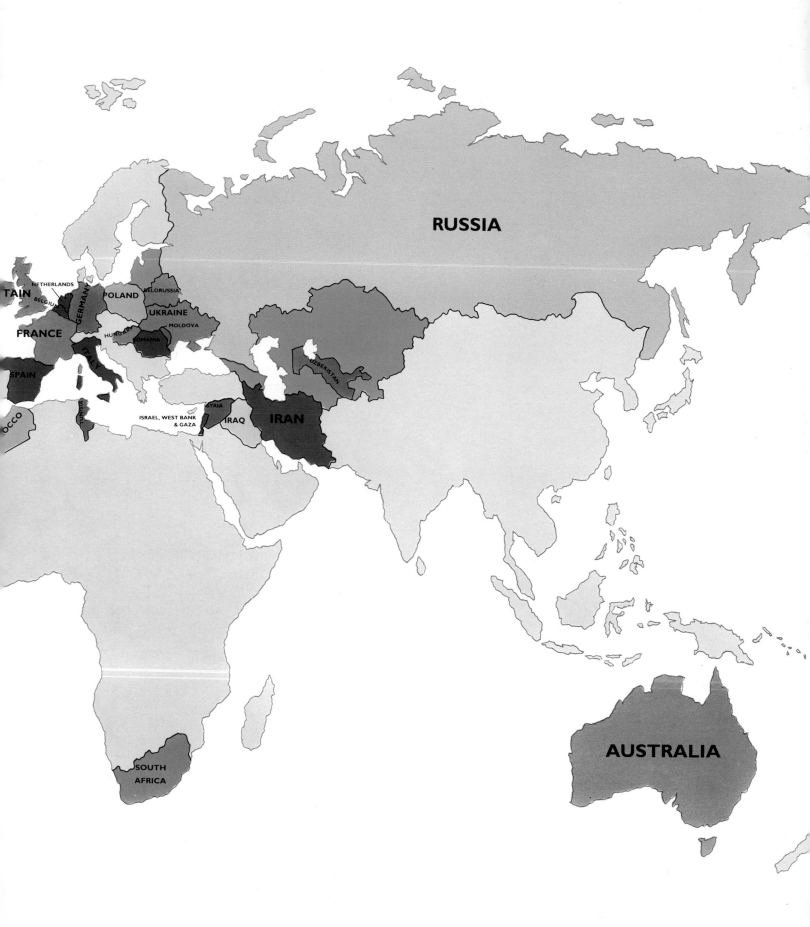

RUSSIA

NETHERLANDS

TAIN

BELGIUM

POLAND

BELORUSSIA

GERMANY

UKRAINE

FRANCE

HUNGARY

MOLDOVA

ROMANIA

UZBEKISTAN

SPAIN

ITALY

IRAN

TUNISIA

OCCO

SYRIA

ISRAEL, WEST BANK
& GAZA

IRAQ

SOUTH
AFRICA

AUSTRALIA

1 Who are the Jewish people?

This book is about the migration of Jewish people over the last 3,500 years. Migration means the movement of people from one place to another. People migrate for many different reasons. They move to find work, or better housing and schools. People also migrate to escape famine, war or other dangerous situations.

There are 14 million Jewish people in the world today. Judaism is the religion of the Jewish people. Anyone who has a Jewish mother can call him or herself Jewish, even if he or she does not practise Judaism. A person can also convert to Judaism.

(Right) A girl lighting the candles on a menorah, the candlestick used for the festival of Hanukkah.

Months		Festivals
Tishri	*(Sept – Oct)*	New Year (Rosh Hashanah) Day of Atonement (Yom Kippur) Feast of Tabernacles (Succot)
Cheshvan	*(Oct – Nov)*	
Kislev	*(Nov – Dec)*	**Festival of Lights (Hanukkah)**
Teveth	*(Dec – Jan)*	
Shevat	*(Jan – Feb)*	New Year for trees (Tu Bishvat)
Adar	*(Feb – Mar)*	Festival of Lots (Purim)
Nisan	*(Mar – Apr)*	Passover
Iyar	*(Apr – May)*	Israel's Independence Day
Sivan	*(May – June)*	Jerusalem Day Feast of Weeks (Shavuot)
Tamuz	*(June – July)*	
Av	*(July – Aug)*	Tisha B'Av, the Ninth of Av
Ellul	*(Aug – Sept)*	

Like Christians and Muslims Jews practise their religion in many different ways. Some live their lives in keeping with Jewish religious customs but many Jewish people are not religious at all.

Religious Jews use their own calendar. They use a Jewish calendar which starts from the date they believe God made the world. This date is 3,760 BCE.

Jews worship in synagogues, and their worship is led by a rabbi. The holy day of the week is the Sabbath, which begins at sunset on a Friday evening and ends an hour after sunset on Saturday. It is a day of rest and peace. Jews who are very religious do not do any kind of work on the Sabbath.

Jews live in almost every country. They are not a racial group, as Jews from different parts of the world look very different. Nearly 30 per cent of all Jews live in Israel, but 45 per cent of Jewish people live in the USA.

Guy Pilavsky

'I'm thirty-two years old and I was born in Tel Aviv, Israel. I now live in London. Over the last century my family has migrated for different reasons. None of us is religious, but we still call ourselves Jews.

'My father's father was born in Chernobyl, Ukraine. He worked on the railways in different parts of Russia. In 1920 he was working in Ekaterinburg, a town in western Siberia. There was a civil war in the Soviet Union at this time. The Tsar had been overthrown by the new Bolshevik government. Also, people were very poor.

'My grandfather decided that he had no future in the Soviet Union. He travelled to Palestine and found work near Jerusalem and then in Tel Aviv.

Guy Pilavsky.

'My mother's grandparents lived in a village in Romania. At this time people were very poor. At the end of the nineteenth century many Jewish people left Romania in search of a better life. My great-grandparents moved the family to Palestine, and then to Egypt, where they became jewellers. My grandmother was born in Cairo, Egypt in 1905.

A market in south Tel Aviv, Israel.

'My mother Dalia was also born in Cairo and grew up speaking French and English. She joined a Zionist youth group, and in 1948 moved to Israel, which had just been formed as the Jewish homeland.

'My parents have lived in Tel Aviv since they got married. But my brother Yuval and I have left Israel. Yuval now lives in Sydney, Australia. I live in London, but I have also lived in New York.' [1]

We can learn about Jewish migration from studying Jewish family names. At various times Jews have changed their family names, or been forced to take new ones. Sometimes this was because they moved to a new country.

Many Jewish people living in eastern Europe did not have European family names until about 300 years ago. Then laws were passed to force Jews to take family names. Some of these names were formed in the same way as British family names. They were based on nicknames, jobs, place names or the first name of an ancestor. For example:

Berliner, named after Berlin in Germany
Minsky, named after Minsk in Russia

Portnoy (Russian) – a tailor
Schneider (German) – a tailor.

In parts of Europe Jewish people had little choice in their new names. They were given them by the police. Often they were given names which reflected how they looked. For example:

Schwarz (German) – black
Klein (German) – small
Gross (German) – big.

In Germany Jewish people were charged a fee for their new family names. Poorer Jews could not afford to pay enough money for a name that sounded nice, and were sometimes given insulting names.

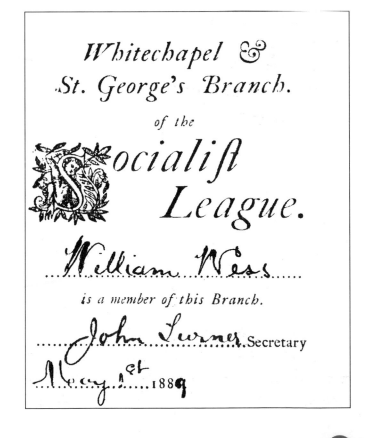

A political party membership card belonging to William Wess. His name came from the word 'Weiss', meaning 'white' in German.

Whitechapel & St. George's Branch.

of the

Socialist League.

William Wess

is a member of this Branch.

John Turner Secretary

May 1st 1889

In some parts of Europe Jews were forbidden to have Hebrew names. So they would choose a European name which had the same meaning as their Hebrew name. For example, Samuel is an English translation of the Hebrew name Shmuel, which means 'God heard'.

When Jewish people migrated they often changed their names. They could translate the name into a new language, or they could use a name which sounded like their real name. For example:

Schneider (German) becomes Taylor in English
Mandel (German) becomes Almond in English
Polak (Polish) becomes Pollock in English.

Some Jewish immigrants had their names altered for them by officials who did not bother to write down their real names. A man called Rosenberg might have his name written down as Rose when he arrived in the USA or Britain.

When Jewish people moved to Israel they were encouraged to take Hebrew names. They often translated their names into Hebrew, for example:

Jung (young in German) becomes Elem in Hebrew
Friedemann (man of peace in German) becomes Shalom in Hebrew.

2 Migration in Biblical times

The Discovery of Moses, *painted by Giovanni Battista (1696–1770).*

It is thought that Abraham was the first Jew. He was born about 3,500 years ago at a place called Ur in Mesopotamia (now in Iraq). In the *Tanach* (Bible) it says that Abraham moved from Ur to a place called Harran. At the age of seventy-five Abraham started on a journey to Canaan (now Israel). Here Abraham promised that he and his family would worship one God. In return God promised to look after Abraham and his descendants, and give them the land now called Israel.

The *Tanach* describes a famine in Canaan. The Jews left for Egypt, where they were taken into slavery. Their life was hard and cruel. The Egyptians so hated the Jews that the Pharaoh (King) ordered that all Jewish baby boys be killed. One child escaped because his mother hid him in a basket by the river. An Egyptian princess found him and took care of him. His name was Moses. It was Moses who led the Jews out of Egypt into the Land of Israel (then known as Canaan) in around 1,250 BCE.

A Yemeni-Jewish family celebrate Passover with a special meal called a Seder.

The story of Moses and the journey to Israel is told in the book of Exodus in the *Tanach*. Every year at Passover Jewish people remember the journey out of Egypt, from slavery to freedom.

According to the *Tanach*, on the way to the Land of Israel God spoke to Moses. He gave the Jews the *Torah* (the first five books of the Bible). The Jews then arrived in the Land of Israel where they fought battles with the people who lived there. They later built a city in Jerusalem.

The stories of Abraham, Moses and David, the King of Israel, may have been altered slightly by storytellers over thousands of years. Archaeologists have found that people did live at Ur, but some believe that the Jews migrated slowly to the Land of Israel rather than making the journeys told in the *Tanach*.

Jews have been called 'Hebrews' and there is a language called Hebrew. The word may come from *kebiru*, meaning traveller. The word Jew comes from 'Judea', the southern part of the Land of Israel. Jews have also been called Israelites.

Solomon, David's son, became king after David's death. After Solomon's death the Land of Israel was divided. Jerusalem became the capital of Judah (Judea). To the north of Judah was the new Kingdom of Israel. Jewish people lived in both countries.

In 722 BCE Israel was attacked by an Assyrian army. Jewish people were taken into exile. Jews lived fairly peacefully in the Land of Judah until 586 BCE. Then the armies of Babylon (now in Iraq) attacked it and destroyed the Temple in Jerusalem. Some 10,000 Jewish families were taken into exile in Babylon. Others returned to Judah. They tried to rebuild the Temple in Jerusalem.

The Jews, led by Judah the Maccabee, fight the army of Antiochus IV. Painted by Matthäus Merian (1593-1650).

The Middle East then came under the influence of the Greeks. The Jews, Turks, and many others all began to learn Greek and wear Greek clothes. Many Jews went to live in the Greek world. Judah was first conquered by the Egyptian Ptolemies. They ruled from 301 BCE to 198 BCE. The Seleucid Turks then ruled Judah. Both the Ptolemies and Seleucids introduced a Greek way of life.

In 168 BCE Antiochus IV, the Seleucid king, tried to stop Jews from observing their customs. The Jews decided to fight the Greeks. One of the Jewish leaders was Judah the Maccabee. His army invaded Jerusalem and freed it from Greek rule. The Jews rededicated the Temple in 164 BCE.

Georgian Jews today. There were Jewish people living all over the Middle East in Greek times, especially in Egypt, Babylon and Tripoli (in modern-day Libya). Iranian, Iraqi and Georgian Jews are today's descendants of people who stayed in Babylon.

3 Rebellion in Roman times

In 63 BCE the Romans invaded the Land of Israel. They made Herod the King of Israel. He was hated by most of his subjects. It was a time of rebellion in the Land of Israel. Jesus lived at this time. Although scholars disagree about his involvement, the Romans saw Jesus as a dangerous Jewish leader. He was killed on the orders of the Roman rulers in 30 CE.

In 66 CE Jewish people in Jerusalem rose up against the Romans and tried to drive them out of the country. Vespasian, the Roman Emperor, sent in a huge army to put down the rebellion. In 70 CE Jerusalem and the Second Temple were destroyed. Most Jewish people fled to other cities in Palestine and hundreds were sent to Rome as slaves. Yet there remained thriving Jewish communities in Yavneh and Galilee. In 147 CE there were big uprisings of the Jewish diaspora. The Jewish diaspora in Egypt was destroyed. The community in Babylon remained and became the centre of the Jewish diaspora.

A model of the siege of Massada. A group of Jews held out against the Romans from 70-73 CE.

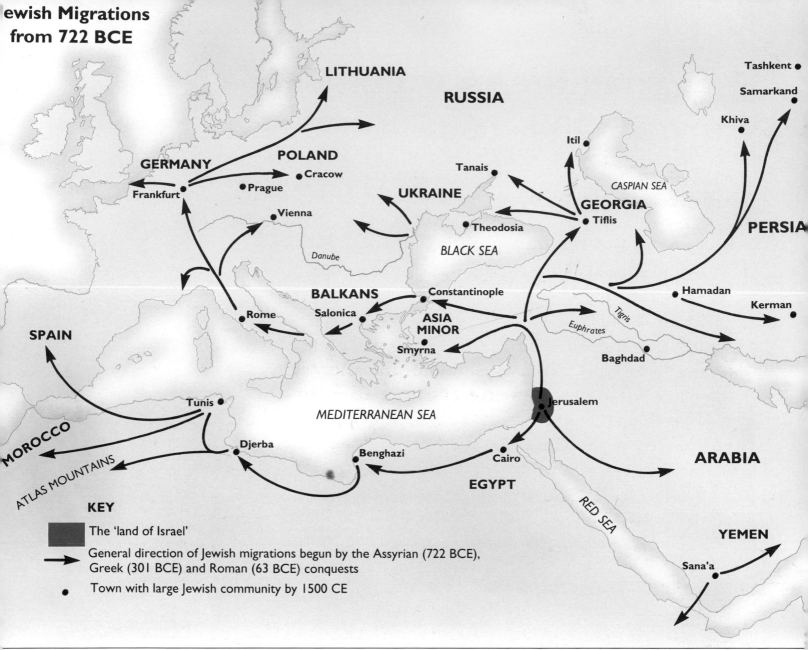

ewish Migrations from 722 BCE

LITHUANIA

RUSSIA

GERMANY
- Frankfurt

POLAND
- Prague
- Cracow
- Vienna

UKRAINE
- Tanais
- Theodosia

Tashkent
Samarkand
Khiva

Itil

CASPIAN SEA

GEORGIA
- Tiflis

PERSIA

Danube

BLACK SEA

BALKANS
- Salonica

Constantinople

ASIA MINOR
- Smyrna

Rome

SPAIN

Hamadan

Kerman

Tigris

Euphrates

Baghdad

MEDITERRANEAN SEA

MOROCCO

Tunis

Djerba

Benghazi

Cairo

Jerusalem

ARABIA

EGYPT

ATLAS MOUNTAINS

RED SEA

YEMEN
- Sana'a

KEY

▮ The 'land of Israel'

→ General direction of Jewish migrations begun by the Assyrian (722 BCE), Greek (301 BCE) and Roman (63 BCE) conquests

• Town with large Jewish community by 1500 CE

In 132 CE Simon Bar Kochba led a Jewish revolt against the Romans. He drove them out of Jerusalem, and held out for three years against the might of Rome. But in 135 CE the Romans destroyed the Jewish forces. Hundreds of thousands of Jews in Judea were killed or forced to flee.

Jews fled to North Africa and to Turkey. They later moved to Spain, Italy, France and Germany.

Women praying at the Western Wall, Jerusalem. This is what remains of the Second Temple.

4 Jewish life in medieval Europe 300–1600

Christianity became the official religion of the Roman Empire in 321 CE. During the next 700 years people in most European countries became Christians. For Jewish people this was a disaster. Hatred against Jews forced them to migrate.

(Above) Anti-Semitic woodcut, 1493, of German Jews killing a Christian boy, and drawing his blood.

(Left) Rioters attack Jewish homes in Frankfurt, Germany, 1614.

Priests in the early Christian Church began to teach that Jews were inferior, and that they were to blame for killing Christ. This was because some Christian leaders still believed that Judaism was a threat to the Christian religion.

Non-Jewish people were encouraged by the Church to believe that Jews practised black magic. Some people also believed that Jews used the blood of children in their Passover meal. Other people blamed Jewish magic for causing the Black Death – bubonic plague, a disease which killed one third of the population of Europe between 1347 and 1350.

The only work that Jews were allowed to do was lending money, or selling clothes and other goods. In medieval Europe most Jews were poor peddlers.

Muslim rulers held Palestine and the Holy City of Jerusalem in the eleventh century. In 1096, 1147–72 and 1189, tens of thousands of Christian soldiers crossed Europe in armies called the Crusades.

In the fourteenth century laws were passed in parts of Europe which made life hard for Jews:

- killing Jews was not a crime;
- Jews had to wear special clothes;
- Jews were not allowed to own land;
- Jews were forbidden to do many jobs.
- Jews were forbidden to join craft guilds.

They wanted to conquer Jerusalem so that the holy places would come under Christian control. On their way to Jerusalem they killed Jews and Muslims, using swords in the shape of the cross.

Jews were also expelled from their home countries. Usually a ruler decided that he could become more popular if he expelled Jewish people, and he passed laws to force them to leave. Between 1096 and 1497 Jews were expelled from most western European countries. Most moved eastwards, to Poland and Lithuania, and to Greece and Turkey.

A crusader in 1097.

Jews in England

The first Jews came to England with William the Conqueror in 1066 (although they may have arrived in smaller numbers with the Romans). By 1200 there were about 3,000 Jews in England, living in London and other towns such as Oxford and Norwich. They had to wear badges to identify them as Jews. Many were bankers to the king. At this time the Church blamed the Jews for the death of Christ. English writers such as Geoffrey Chaucer called Jews 'child murderers'. Jewish people suffered greatly from this hatred.

A woodcut showing the arrest of a rabbi in Lincoln, England in 1255.

A memorial to the Jews of York.

In 1190 many Jews were killed in riots in London, Norwich, Lincoln and York. In York frightened Jews hid in the castle while rioters attacked the outside. After several days the rioters broke into the castle and found the bodies of 150 Jews. They had killed themselves rather than waiting to be murdered.

In 1290 there were hangings of Jewish people. Then the Jewish population of England was expelled by King Edward I. Most Jews went to live in the Netherlands. It was not until 1665 that Jews were allowed to return to England.

Jews in Spain

In eleventh- and twelfth-century Spain Jews had a much better life than most Jews in Europe. Much of southern Spain was ruled by Muslim Arabs. Under Muslim rule Jews were allowed to work in any kind of job. Jewish writers and religious leaders wrote many books.

Part of a mosque in Cordoba, Spain. There are many remains from the time of Muslim rule in Spain.

Jews in Spain spoke Arabic, Spanish and their own Spanish-Jewish language called Ladino. It is similar to Spanish but uses Hebrew script.

Gradually Christian kings conquered Spain. Over the following two hundred years Jews and Muslims were forced to convert to Roman Catholicism. Thousands of them were burnt alive by Christians when they refused. This period of history is known as the Spanish Inquisition.

In 1492 all Jews were expelled from Spain. Over 150,000 Spanish-Jewish refugees fled to North Africa, Turkey, Greece, Palestine and the Netherlands. They took their language with them. Even today Ladino is still spoken by a number of Jews in Turkey, Syria and a few other countries.

Jews of Spanish origin are known as Sephardic Jews. *Sepharad* is a Hebrew word for Spain.

Moses Maimonides, who became a famous religious writer of this period, was born in Spain in the twelfth century.

5 Eastern European Jews 1300–1850

In medieval Europe the land which is now Germany was divided into many small kingdoms. There were large Jewish communities living in them. As in other countries the Jews suffered attacks and hatred. In the twelfth and thirteenth centuries they were expelled from one German kingdom after another. Jewish people gradually moved eastwards after each expulsion, towards Poland, Ukraine and Lithuania.

A nineteenth-century engraving of a synagogue in Lutsk, Ukraine.

Polish and Lithuanian kings welcomed Jewish settlers into their lands. They believed that Jews had useful skills.

Jewish towns and villages grew up all over Poland, Lithuania and the Ukraine. Jewish people usually lived in different villages to their Christian neighbours. These villages were called *shtetlach* (singular *shtetl*). Jews worked as traders, rent collectors, craftsmen, farmers, foresters and innkeepers. Descendants of the medieval German Jews are called *Ashkenazim*.

Life in Poland was peaceful from the fourteenth to the seventeenth century. During this time Polish kings and landowners ruled the Ukraine. But in 1648 the Ukrainians rose up against Polish rule, led by a man named Bogdan Chmielnicki. After defeating the Polish army Chmielnicki and his followers turned against the Jews. They hated the Jews because some had been rent collectors for Polish landlords.

Over a period of three years some 100,000 Jewish people were murdered by Ukrainians. They killed babies and burnt other Jews alive. Many Jewish refugees escaped to Romania or Germany.

During the eighteenth century Jews were again able to live in peace in Poland. But from 1795 Poland and the Ukraine were ruled by the Russian Government, which began to pass laws that made life difficult for the Jews.

YIDDISH

Jewish people spoke their own language called Yiddish. Yiddish is a mixture of different languages. About 70 per cent of the words come from German. Another 25 per cent are from Hebrew. Other words come from French, Polish and Russian. Yiddish is written in the Hebrew script. In 1939, about 10 million people spoke Yiddish, but many Yiddish speakers were murdered in the Second World War. Today Yiddish is still the first language of some religious communities in Europe, the USA and Israel.

A modern Klezmer band. Klezmer music is the traditional Yiddish music of eastern European Jews.

6 The Jewish world in 1850

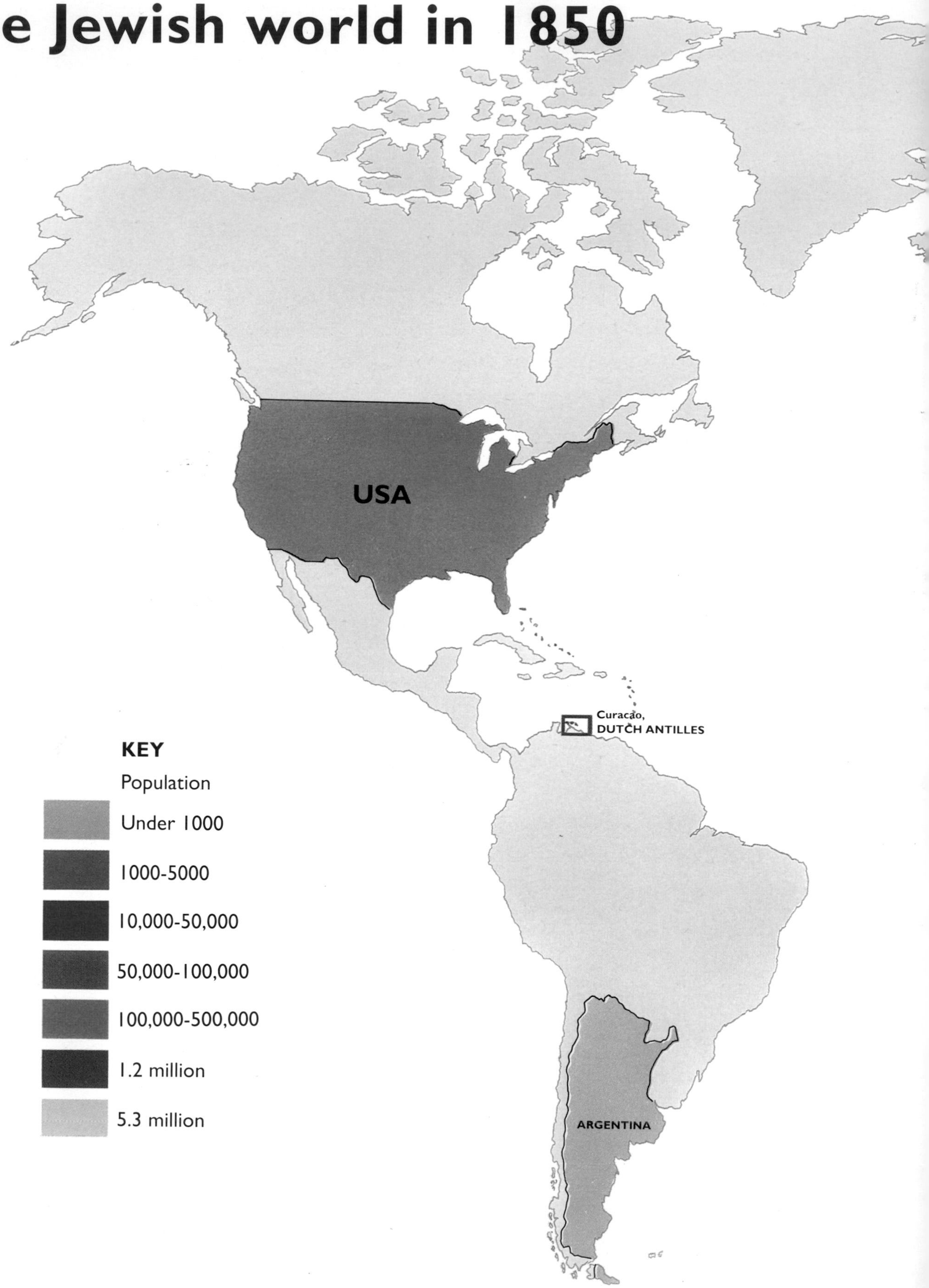

USA

Curaçao,
DUTCH ANTILLES

ARGENTINA

KEY

Population

Under 1000

1000-5000

10,000-50,000

50,000-100,000

100,000-500,000

1.2 million

5.3 million

RUSSIAN EMPIRE

NETHERLANDS
POLAND
GERMAN
CONFEDERATION
GALICIA
SWITZERLAND
AUSTRIA
HUNGARY
ROMANIA
ITALY
BOSNIA
SERBIA
BULGARIA
GEORGIA
GREECE
TURKEY
KURDISTAN
SYRIA AND
LEBANON
PALESTINE
IRAQ
IRAN
AFGHANISTAN
OCCO
TUNISIA
ALGERIA
LIBYA
YEMEN
Bukhara
CHINA
INDIA

7 The great westwards migration 1870–1914

Jewish children in Poland, about 1915.

During the nineteenth century many Jews living in Romania, Austria-Hungary and Russia suffered persecution and poverty. Half of the Jewish population of these countries migrated. Nearly three million Jewish people to moved to the USA, Canada, Britain, Germany and France, and to other European countries.

Life for Russian Jews was the hardest of all. By 1870 about 5.4 million Jews lived in the Russian Empire. Russia was ruled by the Tsar. There were no elections to the Tsar's government. Most Russian people lived in the countryside in great poverty. They were serfs, working on farms owned by a few rich families. Until the nineteenth century most Jewish people lived in the countryside, near their Russian neighbours. They worked as potters, blacksmiths, farmers and rent collectors.

In nineteenth-century Russia poor people were very unhappy with the government and with the landowners. They wanted to own their own land, and have more freedom. The Russian Government blamed the Jews for causing poverty. Rather than blaming landowners for charging high rents to the serfs, it blamed Jewish rent collectors. The Jews became scapegoats.

In 1905 there was a revolution against the Tsar's government but it did not succeed. This picture shows Moscow burning during the revolution.

In 1882 Tsar Alexander III passed the May Laws. Jewish people were not allowed to work on Sundays. They could not travel, and no Jew could own land, work, or live in the countryside.

These laws were particularly bad for Jews living in rural areas. Anti-Semitism increased and there were pogroms against the Jews. Between 1870 and 1914 thousands of Jewish people were killed in pogroms and others injured. The Russian Government deliberately allowed this to happen.

Most Jewish people opposed the Tsar's government. Jewish workers formed trade unions and organized self-defence classes. But the poverty and persecution forced nearly 2.5 million Jewish people from the Russian Empire to move to new countries. They made their way to Hamburg and Bremen, two ports in Germany. Some travelled by train, others walked. The journey was long and hard.

In Hamburg and Bremen they bought boat tickets for London, New York or countries in South America. Here a woman who left Russia in about 1890 remembers what happened:

ROSA LUXEMBURG

Rosa Luxemburg was born in Poland in 1871. She later moved to Germany where she was active in socialist politics and wrote many books and articles. She was murdered in 1919.

A VOICE FROM THE ALIENS

About the Anti-Alien Resolution of the Cardiff Trade Union Congress.

WE, the organised Jewish workers of England, taking into consideration the Anti-Alien Resolution, and the uncomplimentary remarks of certain delegates about the Jewish workers specially, issue this leaflet, wherewith we hope to convince our English fellow workers of the untruthfulness, unreasonableness, and want of logic contained in the cry against the foreign worker in general, and against the Jewish worker in particular.

It is, and always has been, the policy of the ruling classes to attribute the sufferings and miseries of the masses (which are natural consequences of class rule and class exploitation) to all sorts of causes except the real ones. The cry against the foreigner is not merely peculiar to England ; it is international. Everywhere he is the scapegoat for other's sins. Every class finds in him an enemy. So long as the Anti-Alien sentiment in this country was confined to politicians, wire-pullers, and to individual working men, we, the organised aliens, took no heed ; but when this ill-founded sentiment has been officially expressed by the organised working men of England, then we believe that it is time to lift our voices and argue the matter out.

It has been proved by great political economists that a working man in a country where machinery is greatly developed produces in a day twice as many commodities as his daily wage enables him to consume.

'It took eighteen months for my father to save up enough money to send for us...Every day he was worrying about us, and my mother was worrying about him. Of course, it was nothing like what happened later with the Germans, the terror and the killing...But for the time it was an awful experience. And today there are people with the same problems, aren't there?

'Deciding what to take wasn't much of a problem because we had so little. We took some of the boxes and some linen – we didn't know what we were coming to.' [2]

(Above) A leaflet produced in protest at the Aliens Bill, which was intended to stop Jews coming to Britain. It became law in 1905.

Jewish workers in the clothing industry, late nineteenth-century London.

Arrival in Britain

Between 1870 and 1914 over 200,000 Jewish people arrived in Britain. Most of them stayed in Whitechapel, East London. It was a poor area and housing was very bad. It was easy to find work, making shoes, clothing or furniture. But the pay was low and the hours were long. Yet Whitechapel was a very lively place. Some Jews spent their time at the synagogue. Many Jewish immigrants belonged to political organizations. There were anarchists, socialists, communists and Zionists among the Jews of Whitechapel.

Arrival in the USA

About 2 million Jews made their way to the USA between 1890 and 1914. They went in the new steamships which took two weeks to cross the Atlantic. There were up to 2,000 people travelling in each ship, with separate dormitories for single men, single women and families. It was very crowded.

A Russian Jewish woman who went to New York in 1908 remembers that 'the atmosphere was so thick and dense with smoke and bodily odours that your head itched, and when you went to scratch your head you got lice in your hands. There were never enough toilets for the passengers to use'. [3]

The conditions on the ships very gradually improved over the years, and many shipping lines even started to provide kosher food for Jewish passengers.

A family of Russian migrants just after landing in New York.

New migrants arrived at Ellis Island in New York where they were inspected by doctors. Those with serious illnesses were not allowed into the USA and were sent back on the next ship. The luckiest people were those with relatives, already US citizens, eagerly waiting for them at the port.

8 The Nazis in power 1933–45

A Nazi rally in Berlin, Germany, 1938.

The German economy in the 1920s was in a very bad state. By the mid-1920s many businesses were ruined and millions of workers lost their jobs.

The racist Nazi Party, led by Adolf Hitler, offered simple solutions to Germany's problems. The Nazis blamed Jews for ruining the German economy. Once again the Jews became a scapegoat. Hitler told the German people that they were a superior race and one day Germans would rule the world. He said that Germany's problems would be solved when all Jews were removed from the country.

Hitler received huge gifts of money from big businesses. Meanwhile, Nazi thugs attacked and murdered Jews.

In a general election in 1932 the Nazi Party got 37 per cent of all votes. Many German people still opposed the Nazis but they did not work together to stop the Nazis gaining power. Two political parties – the Communist Party and the Social Democratic Party – refused to work with each other to stop the Nazis. They did not realize how dangerous the Nazis were.

In January 1933 other political parties agreed to make Adolf Hitler the Chancellor (head of government). In March 1933 Hitler forced the German parliament to make a law that gave him almost unlimited power. Soon afterwards, he passed new anti-Jewish laws. Jews were not allowed to work as civil servants, teachers, doctors or lawyers. All Jewish businesses had to be marked with a sign.

Between 1933 and 1936 over 220,000 Jewish refugees fled from Nazi Germany. They went to live in British Palestine, the USA, the Netherlands, France and Britain. In March 1938 the Nazis invaded Austria. Many Jews were arrested and sent to concentration camps.

A German-Jewish businessman clearing up after Kristallnacht, *1938.*

ALBERT EINSTEIN

Albert Einstein (1879–1955) was born in Germany and educated in Switzerland. In 1914 he returned to Germany to become director of the Kaiser Wilhelm Physics Institute in Berlin. He won the Nobel Prize for Physics in 1921.

Einstein was forced to leave his job when the Nazis came to power in 1933. He settled in the USA.

In October 17,000 Polish Jews were expelled from Germany. The son of a Polish-Jewish couple among them shot a German diplomat. This was the excuse for a Nazi-led pogrom right across Germany.

On 10 November Jewish homes, synagogues and shops were destroyed, ninety-one people were killed, and more than 30,000 Jews were taken to concentration camps. These riots became known as *Kristallnacht*, or the Night of Broken Glass.

German–Jewish refugee children in a reception camp in Kent, England, 1938.

Before the *Kristallnacht* it had been very difficult for refugees from Nazi Germany to escape to other countries. Even afterwards it was hard. But the British Government did allow 10,000 refugee children to come to Britain. They became known as the *Kindertransporte* (children's transport). Most of them never saw their parents again.

Ron Baker was one of them. He was born in Berlin in 1932, and named Rudi Aschheim. He came to Britain in 1940, one of the last *Kindertransporte* group. He was fostered by the Baker family who lived near Manchester. His father and brother were killed in Auschwitz concentration camp.

'My parents sent me and my brother to the Netherlands for safety. We were looked after by two different families. When Hitler invaded the Netherlands I was put on a boat going to England. It was a boat full of children. As the boat sailed we passed through much fighting and bombing.

'When we arrived we were sent to a church hall near Manchester, in the north of England. The people who looked after us were very kind, but we could not talk to them as we spoke no English. Gradually the church hall emptied, as more and more children went away with foster parents. I was taken by the Baker family, and overnight my name changed from Aschheim to Baker.

'My mother escaped from Germany in 1941. She travelled to Montevideo in Uruguay, where she lived for five years. She was very poor at this time. In 1947 she moved to Palestine. I saw her then, but she was a stranger to me.' [4]

On 1 September 1939 Germany invaded Poland. Britain and France then declared war on Germany, and the Second World War began.

The German Army invading Czechoslovakia, March 1939.

Members of the Hitler Youth Organization burn books by Jewish writers in Salzburg, Austria, 1938.

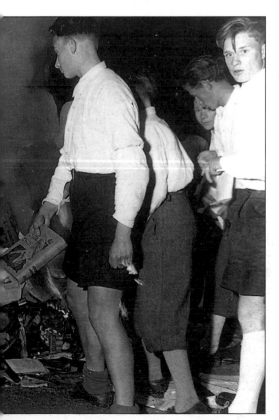

By June 1941 Germany had invaded Czechoslovakia, Poland, Denmark, Norway, the Netherlands, Belgium, France, Yugoslavia, Greece and much of North Africa. The governments of Italy, Hungary, Romania, Bulgaria and Finland were sympathetic to Nazi Germany. Over 7 million Jews were now living in countries that were occupied by Germany, or where their government was friendly towards Germany. Jews were persecuted in these countries.

About 250,000 Polish Jews managed to escape to the Soviet Union. But for most of the Jews there was no escape. Most people in Nazi-occupied Europe were not allowed to travel freely, so it was difficult to escape.

To go to a new country, refugees needed permission from its embassy. But in countries that were occupied by the Nazis, most foreign embassies were closed.

In June 1941 Nazi Germany invaded the USSR. Over 3 million Jews lived in the western part of the Soviet Union. As the German Army marched onwards, special killing units called *Einsatzgruppen* murdered Jews. Within two weeks of invading the Soviet Union, the *Einsatzgruppen* had murdered 800,000 Jews.

In 1942 the Nazis decided to kill Jewish people more quickly. They opened six extermination camps in Nazi-occupied Poland, and between 1942 and 1944 nearly 4 million Jews died in them. About 7 million non-Jewish Poles, Russians, homosexuals, Roma (gypsies), political opponents of the Nazis and disabled people were also murdered in the camps. The British and US Governments knew about the extermination camps but did nothing to stop them.

From 1933–45 over six million Jews were murdered, more than a million of them children. This mass murder is now called the Holocaust.

Children in the Warsaw ghetto. In ghettoes such as Warsaw and Vilna, Jewish people fought to try to stop the Germans taking them to extermination camps.

9 The founding of the State of Israel

ה H	ד D	ג G	ב V	בּ B	א *
כ K	י Y	ט T	ח CH	ז Z	ו V
ע *	ס S	נ/ן ★ N	מ/ם ★ M	ל L	כ/ך ★ CH
שׁ SH	ר R	ק K	צ/ץ ★ TS	פ/ף ★ F	פּ P
★ Letter form at end of word				ת T	שׁ S
* Sound depends on vowel it is used with					

At the end of the nineteenth century Jewish people in eastern Europe were living in poverty and danger. In western Europe Jewish people also suffered anti-Semitism. Theodor Herzl, a young Hungarian Jew, decided that Jews could only be safe in their own country. He and his followers set about founding a Jewish homeland. Not all Jews agreed with Herzl. Jewish socialists argued that it was better to stay and fight anti-Semitism in their own country.

In Switzerland in 1897 Herzl founded the World Zionist Organization. It worked to find a homeland for Jewish people, and soon decided that this should be British Palestine, where there had always been a Jewish community. Any Jew who believed in a Jewish state became known as a Zionist. It was hoped that new Jewish immigrants would come from many different countries. In a future Jewish state Hebrew was to be used.

HEBREW

Hebrew was the language of the Jews from the time of Abraham. It was used less as a spoken language from around 250 BCE, particularly in Europe, but was still used in prayers and the study of Jewish literature. Hebrew remained a mother tongue in North Africa.

A man called Eliezer ben Yehuda devoted his life to modernizing the Hebrew language. He had to find new words for things that did not exist 2,000 years ago and write dictionaries. Today 4.5 million people speak Hebrew.

Between 1881 and 1917 about 60,000 Jews migrated to Palestine. But it was not an empty country. Palestinian Arabs lived there. Some were the descendants of the Philistines, and Arab conquerors who had arrived in the seventh century. They spoke Arabic, and were Muslim or Christian. Palestine was ruled by the Ottoman Empire.

At first the Jews and Arabs lived together as neighbours. But as the numbers of Jewish immigrants increased the Palestinian Arabs began to worry about losing their land.

In 1917 Britain and the Ottoman Empire were at war. Britain captured Palestine. Soon after, the British Government promised Palestine as a national homeland for the Jewish people. At the same time it offered the Arabs freedom from Ottoman rule. So Britain had promised both peoples the same land.

During the 1920s and 1930s Palestinian Arabs rose up against their British rulers and they attacked Jewish settlers. Then Jews started attacking the British and the Palestinians because they regarded Israel as their homeland.

In the 1940s millions of Jews were in danger in Europe. About 100,000 managed to reach Palestine. Violence between Jews and Arabs grew worse. In 1947 Britain said it wanted to leave Palestine, and asked the United Nations (UN) to solve the problem.

Muslims (left), Christians (middle) and Jews (right) in Jerusalem, 1920s.

The UN wanted to divide Palestine into a Jewish state and an Arab state. The Jews accepted the UN plan, but the Arabs rejected it because it meant they would lose their land. The violence continued. British soldiers finally left Palestine on 14 May 1948, and the State of Israel was founded. The dream of Theodor Herzl had come true.

Immediately, the armies of Egypt, Jordan, Syria, Lebanon and Iraq invaded Israel. The war lasted until 1949 when Israel defeated them and increased the size of the country.

A ship carrying refugees from Europe arriving in Palestine, 1946. The banner reads, 'Keep the gates open'.

One of the first laws that the new Israeli Government passed was the 'Law of Return'. This allowed any Jew to come and live in Israel.

GOLDA MEIR

Golda Meir (1898–1978) was born in the Ukraine and educated in the USA. She was a Zionist and in 1921 migrated to Palestine. Meir was active in politics and after the State of Israel was formed, she twice held a cabinet post. She founded the Israeli Labour Party in 1967 and was Prime Minister from 1969–74.

Tunisian Jews in their synagogue in Djerba, 1952.

Between 1948 and 1967 1,157,000 Jewish people migrated from European, African, North American and Asian countries to Israel. Nearly 570,000 Jews left Arab countries such as Morocco, Tunisia, Iraq and Yemen. The Jewish state had been at war with Arab countries, so life became very uncomfortable for Jews who lived in them.

Many Jews also left eastern European countries. Some were survivors of the Holocaust who no longer had homes. Others left because in countries such as the USSR, Poland and Romania Jews were not allowed to practise their religion. Most of the Jews who migrated from Britain and the USA went because they were Zionists.

Eli's story

Eli and Mazal in Tel Aviv, 1993.

'I was born in 1929 in Hodeida, Yemen. My family were religious, and I went to a Jewish religious school. After I left school I got married to Mazal and started working in my father's small shop. Our community in Hodeida lived at peace with our Arab neighbours.

'In the late 1940s life became hard for Jews in Yemen. Some of the synagogues were destroyed and some of our Arab friends turned against us.

Mazal and I felt that Jews had no future in Yemen and we decided to move to Israel. We arrived in 1952, along with many of our Jewish neighbours from Hodeida.

'You can imagine our disappointment when we saw our first home – a tent in a desert camp for new immigrants. We had left behind a big house in Hodeida. We also felt that Jews from Arab countries were not being treated fairly. The European Jews were given better housing – we never saw any of them living in tents!

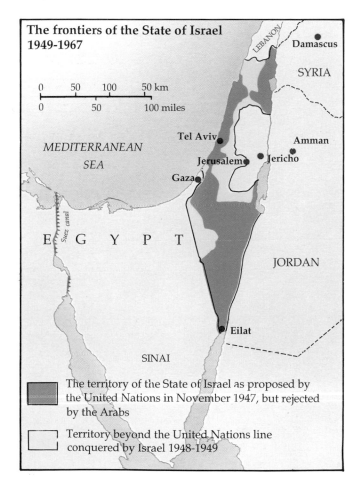

The frontiers of the State of Israel 1949-1967

The territory of the State of Israel as proposed by the United Nations in November 1947, but rejected by the Arabs

Territory beyond the United Nations line conquered by Israel 1948-1949

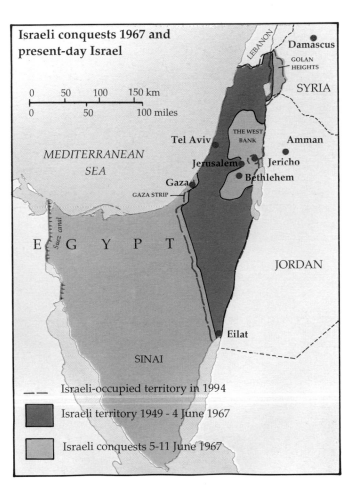

Israeli conquests 1967 and present-day Israel

Israeli-occupied territory in 1994

Israeli territory 1949 - 4 June 1967

Israeli conquests 5-11 June 1967

'Soon we moved from the camp and went to live in a small house in southern Tel Aviv. I found a job in a clothing factory which paid just enough to keep our growing family. Since then we have moved to a new flat in Bat Yam, a town south of Tel Aviv. Life isn't too bad really – we've made Israel our home and our children are happy here. All the Jewish people have now left Yemen so there is no question of us returning there to live.' [6]

10 Migration to Israel after 1967

The migration of Jews to Israel caused a new movement of people. Many Palestinians who already lived there had to leave their homes. In the 1948-9 war 725,000 Palestinians were forced to leave, and after the war between Israel and its Arab neighbours in 1967, 260,000 Palestinian refugees fled to Jordan. After 1967 about 2,600,000 Palestinians were living as refugees in different parts of the world.

Palestinian refugees fleeing to Jordan in 1967.

Yet Jews have continued to migrate to Israel from many different countries. The largest group to arrive since the late 1980s has been Jews from the former USSR. From 1946 to 1987 they were not allowed to practise their religion and very few were allowed to migrate. In 1986 over 2 million Jews lived there.

In 1987 people in the USSR started to be given more freedom by the new government of Mikhail Gorbachev. He allowed more Soviet Jews to emigrate. In 1989 any Soviet Jew who wanted to leave was allowed to do so. Many decided to leave immediately as they wished for a better life in Israel or USA. A lot of Soviet Jews were also frightened by the rising anti-Semitism in the USSR.

Natan Sharansky, a Soviet Jew who was arrested in 1977 for wanting to move to Israel. He was released in 1986 and migrated there.

At first most Soviet Jews went to live in the USA. But at the end of 1989 the USA decided that only 50,000 Soviet Jews would be allowed into the country each year. After this more and more Soviet Jews migrated to Israel.

A Russian-language video shop in Tel Aviv, Israel.

In 1990 more than 170,000 Soviet Jews arrived in Israel and in 1991 about 142,000 moved there. Then the number of Jews going to Israel fell. Many Jews in Russia had heard from friends and relatives that finding a house and a job was becoming very difficult. A few Soviet Jews returned to Russia.

Ethiopian Jews

Over 48,000 Ethiopian Jews were living in Israel in 1994. There are many different stories as to how Jews came to be living in Ethiopia. Many people now believe that there have been Jewish people living there for about 2,000 years. People practising the Jewish religion may have reached Ethiopia from Egypt or from Yemen. In the sixteenth century Ethiopian Jews had their own independent kingdom.

An Ethiopian-Jewish woman in Ethiopia.

For nearly 2,000 years Ethiopian Jews were cut off from other Jewish people. Today their religion is similar to that practised by other Jews 2,000 years ago.

Ethiopian Jews lived in Gondar, in the north-west of Ethiopia. Most of them were farmers. They were poor and they also faced anti-Semitism. Just as in medieval Europe the Ethiopian Jews were accused of practising black magic, and of being responsible for killing Jesus.

The first Ethiopian Jews arrived in Israel in the 1970s, where they were welcomed. Most of them left Ethiopia and travelled to Sudan. They then caught planes and boats to Israel. By 1983 4,000 Ethiopian Jews had arrived.

Between 1983 and 1985 Ethiopia was hit by two famines, caused by drought and war. Over 6 million people fled from their homes to try and find food. Some 500,000 died of starvation. Ethiopian Jews joined with their Christian neighbours and fled to Sudan. Most Ethiopian Jews went to a refugee camp called Um Raquba. Over 4,000 died on the way or in the camp.

The Israeli Government decided to bring the Jewish refugees to Israel. With the help of the US Government, it organized a secret transport of Ethiopian Jews in November 1984. Over 15,000 Ethiopian Jews were taken by land, air and sea.

Ethiopian Jews arriving in Israel in 1990 being reunited with relatives who came earlier.

In May 1991, when there was a civil war in Ethiopia, the Israeli Government rescued the remaining Jews. 14,000 were taken to Israel by aeroplane within thirty-six hours. The rescue mission was called 'Operation Solomon'.

In Israel the Ethiopian Jews can buy good food. There are excellent schools and hospitals. But there are also difficulties. Some religious Jews refuse to accept the Ethiopians as Jews because their ways of worship are different. They have black skin and look different from most Israeli Jews so they sometimes face racist attacks and insults. Many Ethiopian Jews have also found it difficult to find work.

Reuven Menashe describes how he came to Israel in 1984 as part of Operation Moses:

Ethiopian-Jewish children learning Hebrew prayers.

'My family used to live in a village in Gondar. At the end of 1983 there was no food in the village. We sold everything to try and raise money to buy food. But when our animals and jewellery were gone we knew we had to leave. I can remember the adults in the village meeting at night to discuss the journey to Sudan. As children we were quite excited.

'We walked for about five weeks. Many people died on the journey, including my younger brother. My legs hurt a lot. We reached Sudan and stayed in a camp – then my parents said we would be going to Israel. We travelled in a plane without seats.

'When we first arrived we stayed in a reception centre. Here we found out about life in Israel and started to learn Hebrew. After a few months my family moved to a new flat in Dimona, a town in southern Israel. My father hasn't found a job, and he's always depressed. Not all the neighbours are friendly. Some of them look down on us because we're from Africa. But I'm happy here, I like my school and next year I'm going in the army.' [7]

11 The Jewish diaspora

Today about 9,200,000 Jews live outside Israel (see map pages 4–5). They live in almost every country of the world. Jewish people who live outside Israel are known as the Jewish diaspora. The word 'diaspora' comes from a Greek word meaning 'scattered'. Jewish people are scattered in many countries.

Helen Suzman, a Jewish South African who campaigned against apartheid.

CHARLES SAATCHI

Charles Saatchi was born in 1943, the son of Iraqi Jews who left Baghdad. He is the director of one of Britain's largest advertising agencies, and also has an art collection.

Jewish people continue to migrate for many different reasons. In 1992 about 500 Jewish refugees fled from fighting in Bosnia, in the former Yugoslavia. Jews have continued to leave Russia, and in 1993 the Israeli Government helped the last Jews to leave Yemen.

Here are some stories of Jewish people around the world. Some have themselves migrated, or they come from families who have migrated.

A Jewish-American woman.

Kimberley

'I'm twenty-six years old and I live in San Francisco, USA. My great-grandparents came to the USA from Poland and Czechoslovakia at the beginning of this century. One of my great-grandfathers was very active in the *Bund* in Poland – a Jewish trade union. I'm very proud of his work.

'I've moved homes many times in my life. My parents were university teachers, so we moved when they changed jobs. I left home at eighteen and went to university to study psychology. Now I work in a bank.

'I'm not at all religious. I love pork sausages and other food which is not kosher. But I always go back home to celebrate Rosh Hashanah and Passover with my family. I think it's important to keep traditions alive. Recently I've joined a group of young Jews who are learning Yiddish. I'd like to marry a Jewish man, but I just haven't met the right one yet!' [8]

Jessica

'I'm thirty-four and I come from Chile. My grandparents came from the Ukraine, Spain and Macedonia.

Children celebrate the festival of Purim at a Jewish day school, England.

'I grew up in Santiago, the capital of Chile. In 1973 a military coup overthrew the democratic government and General Pinochet came to power. More than a million refugees fled Chile during the following years. My family travelled by boat to Britain. I had to learn a new language in school, so now I'm bilingual – I'm fluent in English and Spanish.

'After the government changed in Chile, my dad went back there, but the other members of my family have stayed here. I also have relatives in Israel. I'd like to stay in Britain – it was hard enough leaving Chile and I don't want to leave my friends behind and start a new life again. [9]

Prisoners in Santiago stadium after the military coup. Many people were killed by the army under Pinochet's dictatorship.

Gita

'I'm eleven years old. Until last year I lived in Tehran, the capital of Iran. Now my family lives in Sydney, Australia. We left Iran because my dad could not get promotion in his job as a doctor. My parents believed that this was because he is Jewish.

'Now my dad has a good job in a hospital. I go to a Jewish primary school where I learn Hebrew as well as English. I love it when there is a Jewish festival – we celebrate all the festivals at home and at school.' [10]

Glossary

Anarchist A person who believes that governments should not rule over people. In parts of Russia and in the Jewish East End of London between 1880 and 1914 many Jewish workers supported anarchist political groups.

Anti-Semitism Hostility or violence towards Jewish people. Anti-Semitism is a form of racism.

Ashkenazi Jew A Jew whose family descends from medieval Germans.

Canaan A name used at the time of Abraham and Moses for the land which is now Israel.

Communist Someone who believes that the ownership of land and factories should be shared.

Convert To become a member of a different religion.

Diaspora Jewish people who live outside Israel.

Expulsion The forced removal of people from a country.

Ghetto An area of a town or city in which Jews were forced to live. The word 'ghetto' comes from an Italian word.

Hebrew The language of the Jewish people from 3,500 BCE to 250 BCE, and now the language of the State of Israel.

Holocaust The murder of 6 million Jews by the Nazis from 1933–45. The Hebrew word *Shoah* is also used by many Jews.

Israel The Land of Israel is described in the Old Testament of the Bible. It included modern Israel and the West Bank of the River Jordan. The modern State of Israel was formed in 1948.

Jerusalem The capital of the ancient land of Israel, of Palestine and of modern Israel. It is a holy city for Muslims, Christians and Jews.

Judaism The religion of the Jews.

Kibbutz A community of Israelis who share the ownership of land and small factories.

Kosher food Food which is prepared in a special way according to Jewish religious laws.

Palestine The Roman name for the land which is now Israel and the West Bank and Gaza Strip.

Palestinian Arab A person whose family comes from the land called Palestine before 1948. Most Palestinian Arabs are Muslim and the rest are Christian.

Passover The Jewish festival which marks the return of the Jews from exile in Egypt. It is also called Pesach.

Pogrom An attack on a particular group of people, especially Jews in nineteenth-century eastern Europe, allowed by the government.

Rabbi A spiritual leader of the Jewish community.

Racism Hostility or violence towards a group of people because of the belief that they are inferior. Anti-Semitism is a form of racism.

Refugee Someone who has fled a country because his or her life is in danger.

Sabbath In Judaism, the day of the week for rest and prayer. It starts at sunset on Friday and ends an hour after sunset on Saturday.

Scapegoat A person or a group of people blamed for problems which they did not cause.

Sephardic Jew A Jew whose family came originally from Spain or Portugal.

Shtetl (plural *Shtetlach*) A Jewish village or small town in eastern Europe.

Temple Jewish place of worship. The Jewish Temple was where sacrifices were brought before God during festivals and other occasions.

Yiddish The language of most eastern European Jews until 1945.

Yom Kippur The Day of Atonement, the holiest day of the year for religious Jews. They fast and ask God to forgive their sins.

Zionism A political idea developed by Theodor Herzl, a Hungarian Jew. Zionists worked to create a state for Jewish people – Israel. Zionists today believe that all Jews have the right to live in the State of Israel.

Find out more

BOOKS TO READ

For teachers

Encyclopaedia of Jewish History (Facts on File Inc, Massada, Israel, 1992)

A Historical Atlas of the Jewish People by Eli Barnavi (Hutchinson, 1992)

Winter in the Morning by Janina Bauman (Pavanne, 1986)

Jew Boy by Simon Blumenfeld (Lawrence and Wishart Ltd, 1986)

Tales of Rabbi Nachman by Buber (Souvenir Press, 1974)

Atlas of Jewish History by Dan Cohn-Sherbok (Routledge, 1994)

East End Jewish Radicals 1875-1914 by William Fishman (Duckworth, 1975)

The Holocaust: The Jewish Tragedy by Martin Gilbert (Fontana, 1986)

A Jewish History Atlas by Martin Gilbert (Dent, 1993)

A Century of Ambivalence: Jews of Russia and the Soviet Union by Zvi Gitelman (Viking, 1988)

The Jewish People by Goldberg and Rayner (Penguin, 1993)

The Nazi Holocaust by Ronnie Landau (I. B. Tauris, 1992)

A Death Out of Season by Emanuel Litvinoff (Penguin, 1973)

The Joys of Yiddish by Leo Rosen (Penguin, 1968)

The Russians in Israel by Naomi Shepherd (Simon and Schuster, 1993)

'They fought back': Jewish Resistance in the Holocaust by Y. Suhl (Schocken Books, New York, 1976)

From Prejudice to Genocide: Learning About the Holocaust by Carrie Supple (Trentham, 1993)

Israel: the Oriental Majority by Schlomo Swirski (Zed Press, 1989)

Minority Rights Group Reports
The Falashas: Jews of Ethiopia
The Jews of Africa and Asia
Israel's Oriental Immigrants and Druzes

For students

Jewish Festivals by Jane Cooper (Wayland, 1989)

Chika the Dog in the Ghetto and *What Happened in the Shoah?* by Batshevan Dagan, Auschwitz survivor. Written in rhyme. (Kay Tee Inc, 1992/3)

Palestine and Israel (Oxfam/Refugee Council 1991)

Anne Frank: The Diary of a Young Girl (Pan, 1952) and Anne Frank pack (available from Eastside Books Ltd, 178 Whitechapel Rd, London E1 1BJ)

The Other Way Round by Judith Kerr (Armada Books, 1983)

When Hitler Stole Pink Rabbit by Judith Kerr (Armada Books, 1974)

Jewish Culture by Jenny Wood (Franklin Watts, 1988)

USEFUL ADDRESSES

Holocaust Education Trust
BCM Box 7892
London WCIN 3XX
tel. 071 222 6822

Institute of Jewish Affairs
7 Hertford Street, London W1M 7DD Tel. 071 388 4525

Irish-Jewish Museum
3-4 Walworth Rd
Dublin 8
tel. Dublin 531797

The Jewish Museum
Woburn House, Upper Woburn Place, London WC1H 0EP
tel. 071 388 4525
The museum contains a collection of objects illustrating Jewish life and worship. In the same building is the Jewish Lecture and Information Committee.

The London Museum of Jewish Life
The Sternberg Centre, 80 East End Road, London N3 2SY
tel. 081 346 2288
The Museum is open from Sundays to Thursdays. It organizes lectures, guided walks of Jewish London, publishes research and has an outreach programme to schools. It also has videos about Jewish life in Britain and displays which can be hired.

Manchester Jewish Museum
190 Cheetham Hill Road, Manchester M8 8LW. Tel. 061 834 9879
This museum has an education department.

Minority Rights Group
379 Brixton Road, London SW9 7DE. Tel. 071 978 9498

Springboard Education Trust
32 Foscote Road, London NW4 3SD. Tel. 081 202 7147

The Wiener Library
4 Devonshire Place, London W1M 2BH. Tel. 071 636 7247
The library contains books and documents about the Holocaust and anti-Semitism.

Yakar Library
2 Egerton Gardens, London NW4 4BA. tel. 081 202 5551
Jewish lending library.

Notes on sources

1 Author interview, 1993
2 Jewish East End Education Pack, 1988
3 Ellis Island, The Official Souvenir Guide by B. Colin Hamblin, Companion Press, Santa Barbara, California
4 Author interview, 1989
5 Author interview, 1993
6 *Ibid*, 1993
7 *Ibid*, 1993
8 *Ibid*, 1993
9 *Ibid*, 1993
10 *Ibid*, 1993
11 *Ibid*, 1993

Source for map on p15: *Atlas of Jewish History* by Dan Cohn-Sherbok (Routledge, 1994)

Index

Entries in **bold** indicate subjects shown in pictures as well as in the text.
'M' stands for migration.

PICTURE ACKNOWLEDGEMENTS: Archiv für Kunst und Geschichte 11, 13 (left), 16 (below), 24, 28, 32; Camera Press 15, (B Whitaker) 35, 45; Eye Ubiquitous (J Burke) imprint & contents page, (B Harding) 19 (both), (TRIP) 44 (above); Sonia Halliday 10; Robert Harding 31 (above), (D Holden) 40; Hulton 29 (both), 30 (above), 34 (both), 36 (above); John Massey Stewart 13 (right); Museum of the Jewish Diaspora, Tel Aviv 20; Museum of Jewish Life 26; John Nathan 21; Popperfoto 25 (below); Rex Features 43 (below); Ann Ronan 16 (above), 17 (below), 18 (above); Topham 14, 25 (above), 27, 30 (below), 38, 39 (above), 41, 42; Wayland (Z Mukhida) cover & title page, (M Dent) 7 (above), R Neu: 7 (below), 8, 36 (below), & 39 (below); York Archaeological Trust 18 (below); Zefa 12 (above), 44 (below). Artwork: Jenny Hughes 6; Peter Bull 4-5, 15, 22-3 and 37.